Tulipán

the Puerto Rican giraffe

written by Ada Haiman

illustrations by Atabey Sánchez-Haiman

Tulipán, the Puerto Rican Giraffe

c Text: Ada Haiman
c Illustrations: Atabey Sánchez-Haiman

PMB 108
701-1 Ponce de León Avenue
San Juan, Puerto Rico 00907

iaiahaiman@gmail.com
ash@giraffesandrobots.com
GIRAFFESandROBOTS.com
JIRAFASyROBOTS.com

First edtion: 2013

ISBN-10:0615924085

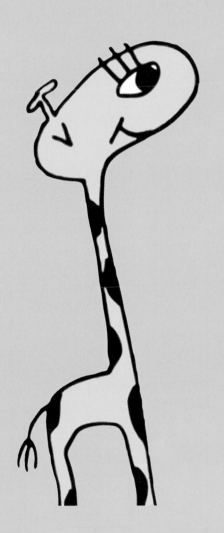

DEDICATION

Written for my daughter, whose giraffe prints were not accepted at the gift shop of the Puerto Rican Museum of Contemporary Art in 2004 because "giraffes were not Puerto Rican;" they unabashedly recommended she paint coquis.

Dedicated to all those who have come from all over the world to settle. live, breathe, grow and work productively in Puerto Rico.

A special thanks to Tere Marichal for her support and encouragement.

To my dear León.
To Roberto, thank you.

AH

To Kian Milo, my little T. Rex. TQM

ASH

This is the story of Tulipán, the Puerto Rican giraffe.

Tulipán was a happy giraffe who roamed around The Bronx (that's in New York City) getting into mischief with her friends.

She often spent the summer with her grandmother, so she had another set of friends to hang out with in the mountain town of Aibonito (that's in Puerto Rico).

Some people, when they met her for the first time, would say: "You don't look Puerto Rican."

When she heard this, Tulipán
would scratch her head and think:

"You don't look Puerto Rican?
What exactly does that mean?"

She puzzled over this strange statement and wondered,

"Could it be...

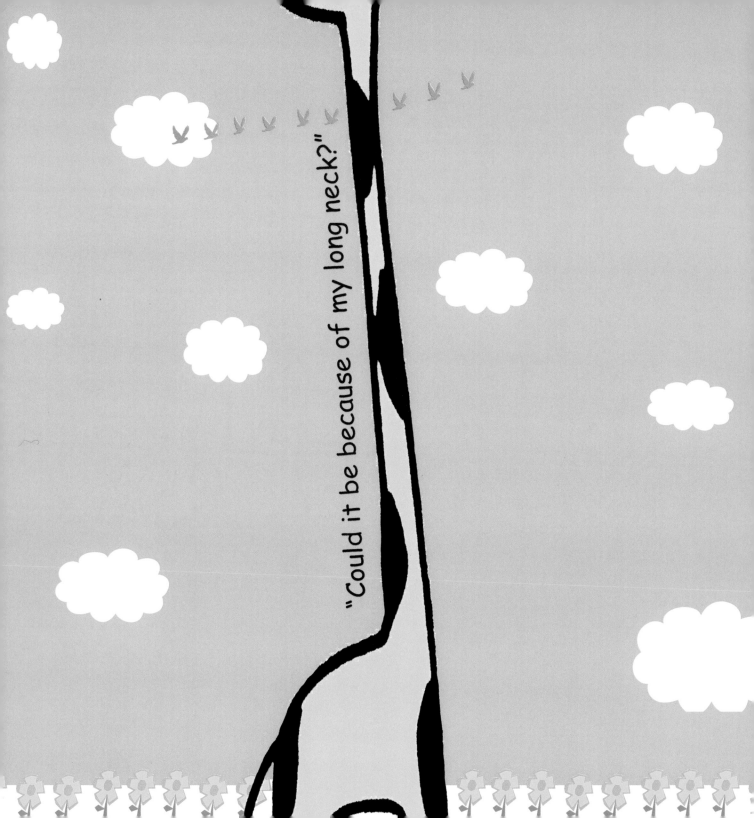

She thought and thought and thought about this for a very long time.

"What does it mean to be Puerto Rican?"

She knew she was not born in Puerto Rico, but she figured that couldn't be so important, especially when 4,000,000 Puerto Ricans lived off the island.

N

W   E

S

NYC

Until, one day, she came to the conclusion
that what was really and truly important was
that she had lived...

She had lived hearing stories about and visiting the sunny, enchanted island washed by the seas.

She had lived swept away by syncopated rhythms.

(She also enjoyed classical music.)

She had lived riding the airbus between her two homes.

(It was fun being of two places: one cold, one hot, one city, one country; these contrasts fired her imagination.)

She had lived marked by the plantain stain.

(That was what her mother always said and,
although she didn't know precisely what it meant,
the way her mother said it made her feel real good.)

She had lived speaking a living and breathing Spanish.

(Of course, she spoke English too.)

Some of her favorite words were:

Bodega el tomate

That's the roof of the building.

el rufo

la marketa

That's where Tulipán and her family would shop for all kinds of stuff cheaper than at the mall.

That's satisfaction,
peace and agreement
all rolled up in one word.

It is always said with a smile.

chévere

guagua

Her friend from Chile would correct her: "Autobús, Tuli, autobús."

But Tulipán loved the unique and familiar sound of the word *guagua*.

pegao

That's the crispy rice that's stuck to the bottom of the pot.

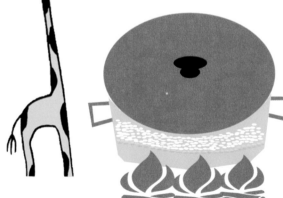

That was how her mother described
the mess in Tulipán's room.

revolú

el choliseo

A coliseum built and a word coined in honor of José Miguel Agrelot, our Don Cholito.

Hot, greasy and finger-licking good soul food.

cuchifritos

That's the corner grocery store, where they could buy on credit or *fiao*.

bodega

When they were hungry but had no money, her mother would say: "Tuli, *go to la bodega* and get some rice and beans, *fiao*."

When you leave metropolitan San Juan and go inland, that's called "going to the island," although it is all part of the same island. If you are not Puerto Rican, that can be confusing.

la isla

That's the University of Puerto Rico, la UPR.

la iupi

A great word! It may sound like a song, but it hurts when you get hit on the head.

cocotazo

sancocho

chiringa

A kite.

coquí
coquí
coquí

A tiny little frog with a great big voice. It made Tulipán feel powerful.

coquí

And the best word of all...

niuyorrican

It simply means, there can be more than one you.

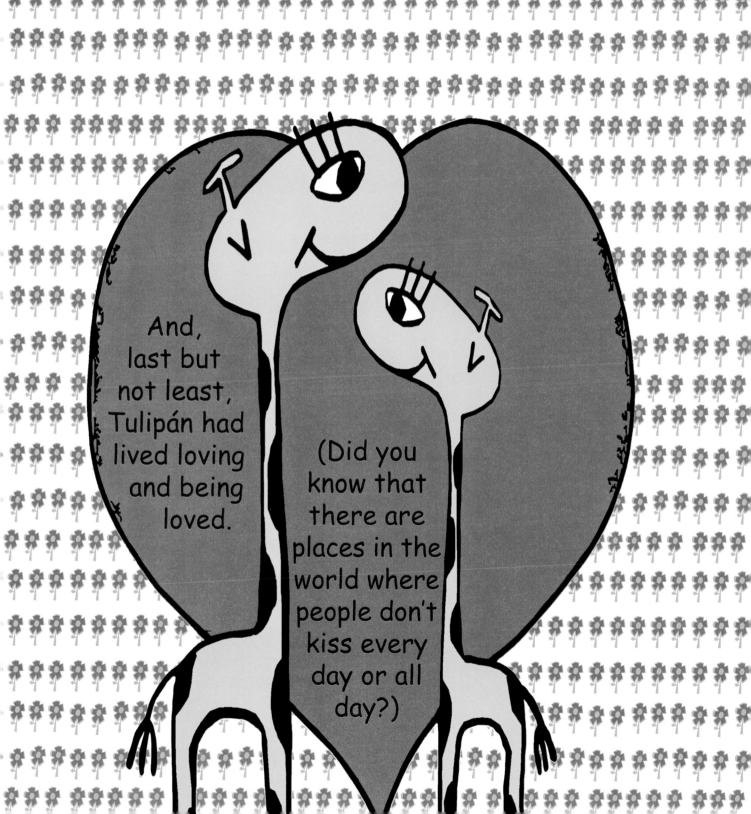

chévere

So, once she had figured this puzzle out, when people said to her: "You don't look Puerto Rican," Tulipán would just smile and answer, "Chévere," because she knew that was NOT important.

What do you think?

Can a giraffe be Puerto Rican?

yes   no

And she lived happily ever after.

Made in the USA
Columbia, SC
21 June 2021